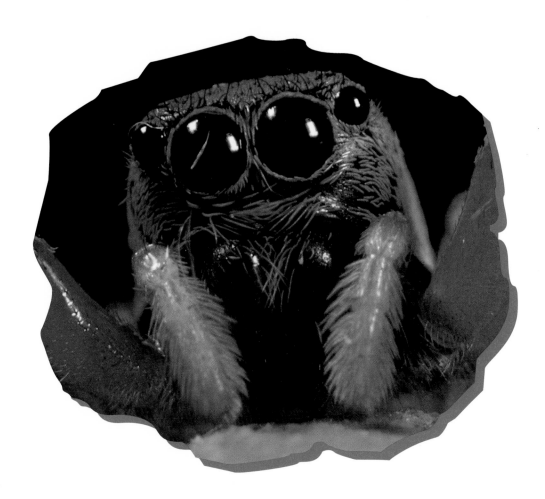

A GOLDEN BOOK • NEW YORK

Golden Books Publishing Company, Inc., New York, New York 10106

Created by Two-Can for Golden Books Publishing Company, Inc. Copyright © 1998 Golden Books Publishing Company, Inc. All rights reserved.
Printed in the USA. No part of this book may be reproduced or copied in any form without written permission from the copyright owner.
GOLDEN BOOKS®, A GOLDEN BOOK®, TOTALLY AMAZING™, and G DESIGN™ are trademarks of
Golden Books Publishing Company, Inc. Library of Congress Catalog Card Number: 98-84145
ISBN: 0-307-20160-0   R MCMXCIX

Creepy-crawly Spiders!

Are you nervous about spiders? Well, don't worry! Most of them are much happier munching on insects than nibbling on you. So get ready—you are about to enter the totally amazing world of spiders!

Spider Breakdown

There are many different kinds of spiders, but they all have the same basic body parts. They have: a body made up of a head, thorax, and abdomen; eight spindly legs; a pair of razor-sharp fangs for biting prey and fighting; and spinnerets, for spinning those amazing webs.

A SPIDER FLAT ON ITS BACK

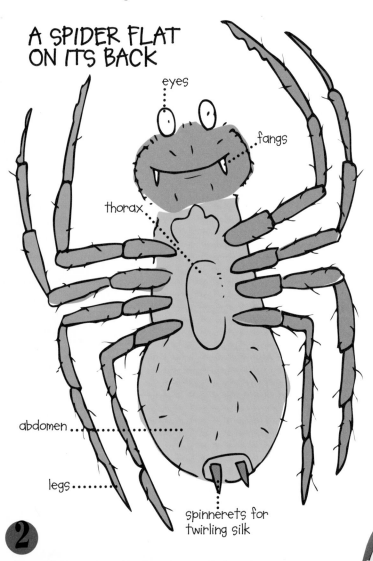

eyes

fangs

thorax

abdomen

legs

spinnerets for twirling silk

What's in a Name?

Spiders belong to a bunch of animals called arachnids. Arachne was the name of a girl in an ancient Greek story who beat the goddess Athena at a weaving contest, so Athena changed her into a spider.

Just my luck!

Where in the World?

Spiders live everywhere on Earth, except Antarctica. They make their homes under rocks and logs, in tunnels and trees, and also underwater. Spiders have been rocketed into space to see if they still spin webs without gravity. They do!

Strange but True

Most spiders have eight eyes. Some spiders have six, four, or two eyes, and some have no eyes at all!

▲ A tiny crab spider changes its color slowly to match the color of the flower where it sits. It waits in ambush for a passing insect!

Home Sweet Home

Spiders build incredible homes, from cozy burrows to underwater bubble houses. Many spiders rig their homes with traps and trip wires to capture prey.

Cool Living

How does a hairy tarantula stay cool in the sizzling desert heat? It digs a deep bunker in the sand. The underground den keeps the spider nicely chilled until the sun goes down and the air turns cooler. Only then will it creep outside to find a bite to eat or a mate for the evening.

It's a Trap

The spider in the photograph has rigged up trigger threads around the outside of its nest. If an insect disturbs the threads, the spider will know a tasty meal is nearby.

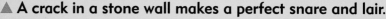 A crack in a stone wall makes a perfect snare and lair.

Cave spiders are excellent at rock climbing. They have extra-strong, long legs to help them grip and climb up the steep walls of their caves.

Spider Cities

Social spiders work together in construction teams to build enormous spider cities. The spiders connect huge sheets of webs, making a giant web big enough to cover a tree. The spiders also hunt together in groups so that they can catch and share larger prey.

UNDER CONSTRUCTION

Watery Homes

A water spider builds its home underwater. It weaves a silk platform. Then it traps an air bubble from the surface and attaches it to the platform. When the air begins to run out, the spider pops up to the surface for another bubble.

Almost home.

Knock, Knock

The secretive trapdoor spider lives in a tunnel with a tightly fitting door. When visitors approach, it opens the door and eats them!

▲ A trapdoor spider is an expert decorator. It makes sure that its burrow is waterproofed with soil, then it adds a soft coating of spit and silk.

Waiting Game

The spider spends many evenings at home, waiting patiently below its door, sometimes with its front legs just sticking out. When the spider feels the vibrations of passing prey, it rushes out, grabs and bites the prey, and drags it into the burrow. Then the spider firmly bangs the door shut.

That's Weird

One kind of trapdoor spider plugs the top of its burrow with its hard, flat belly, which fits snugly into the hole, just like a cork in a bottle. Now it's safe from enemies.

Good evening!

Super Spinners

Spider-silk is tough, light, and elastic, so it's perfect for lassoing prey, making a comfortable bed, a dangerous trap, or a rope swing to escape from danger.

Spinning Silk

Spiders spin different kinds of silk for different jobs! When the spider first spins the silk, it is liquid, but it soon hardens into thread that can be stronger than steel.

SILK FOR KEEPING EGGS SAFE

SILK FOR DRAGLINES

SILK FOR WEBS

SILK FOR WRAPPING PREY

Look, I'm Tarzan!

What a Drag!

A spider can always make a getaway. Wherever a spider roams, it leaves a trail of thin silk thread, called a dragline, which works just like a rope swing. When the spider is threatened, it jumps on to the dragline and swings to safety.

Under the Microscope

This picture has been magnified many times. It shows silk being spun from tiny tubes on the spider's body.

Sticky Habit

A spider's web is not sticky all over. A spider doesn't get caught in its own web because it avoids the sticky threads. It also coats its body with slippery oil so that the silk doesn't stick.

Strange but True
Spiders are good at pest control. Without spiders, the world would be overrun with insects.

▲ A spider keeps its prey hidden from other hungry mouths by wrapping it up in a ball of silk.

Web Masters

No one teaches a spider how to spin a web—it just knows! Different spiders spin webs in all kinds of shapes and sizes, including ones that look like big string bags, bicycle wheels, and hammocks.

In the Net

A net-throwing spider knits together silk to make a hand-held web. It doesn't sit on its web like other spiders, but holds the web in its two outstretched front legs. When an unsuspecting insect walks below, the spider stretches the net out wide and drops it over the victim's body.

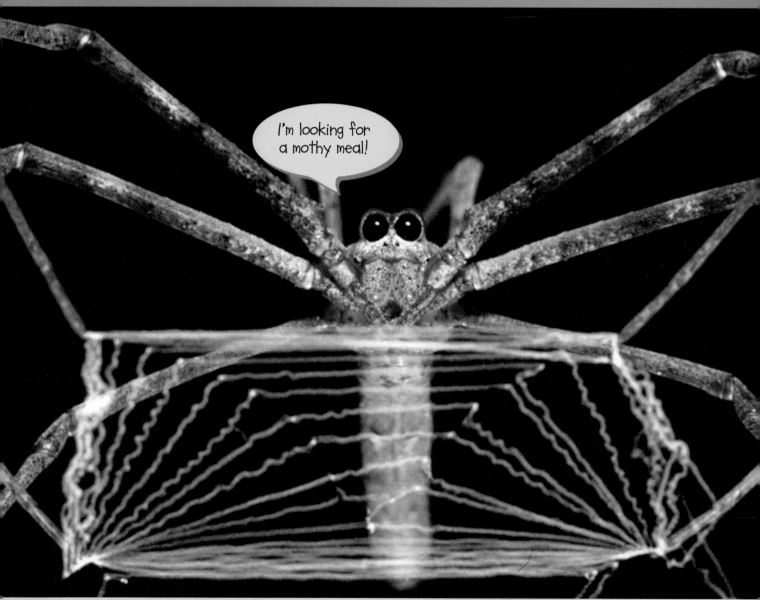

I'm looking for a mothy meal!

▲ A net-throwing spider's web is stretchy enough to catch and wrap up a big moth.

ORB SPIDER'S WEB

A speedy spider spins a silk bridge between two twigs...

Whee!

...then parachutes down to add supporting threads.

It spins threads from the middle to the edge, in the shape of bicycle spokes on a big wheel.

Over and under, in and out, and back again.

Then, the spider spins from the middle outward. It goes round and round.

This part always makes me dizzy!

Finally, it spirals back to the middle of the web. This time, it lays a sticky thread to catch its dinner.

Orb Webs

Every night, most orb spiders spin a bouncy web, which contains enough thread to make a pair of silk tights. The web is light enough to blow in a breeze but extremely strong. It must be strong enough to hold the spider, which is 4,000 times heavier than its web.

That's Weird

A spider's web is packed with healthy nutrients. Before a spider spins a new web, it makes a nice big meal out of the old one!

Mmm, web again... delicious!

Horrible Hammocks

The hammock weaver spider has a cunning plan. It spins a flat or slightly domed net of silk. Above the net, it sets up a mass of tangled lines to knock flying insects on to the net, or hammock, below. Then, the spider rests and waits for an insect to fly along and land in the hammock for its next meal!

On the Prowl

Many spiders are fierce warriors. They go out on patrol, ready to hunt down and attack creatures that wander into their paths. Others leap on to their victims, glue them to the spot with sticky spit, or even worse...

Jumping Around

The jumping spider has huge eyes that swivel around like telescopes to detect movement. It creeps up on its prey, then it jumps, opening its jaws mid-flight to deliver a lethal bite when it lands.

Strange but True
A jumping spider can see its prey from a long way off—over 14 times its body length!

▲ A jumping spider is a champion long-jumper. It crouches down like a cat, pushes on its back legs, then propels itself forward.

What's in a Name?

The spitting spider is named after its disgusting habit of spraying prey with two streams of gruesome goo. This goo causes the prey to fall to the ground. The spider has plenty of time to stroll over and kill it.

Spider Burglars

A few kinds of spiders are expert thieves that steal from other spiders' webs. The burglar spider moves quietly and unseen over another spider's web, nibbling up old scraps of food. When it is really brave, it eats the main prey, too.

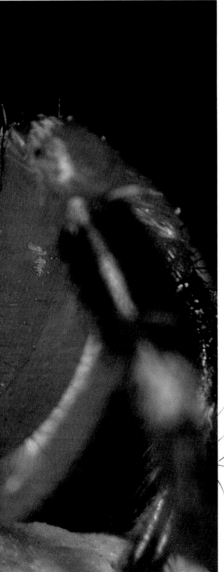

Soon you'll be mine!

On your marks...

A wolf spider is a large and hairy athlete. It can look for prey in four directions at once. When it sees something, it sprints off with deadly accuracy.

The fishing spider spends its days dangling its front legs in ponds. When it picks up ripples made by a struggling insect that has fallen in, it grabs the unlucky creature and reels in its supper.

▽ The wandering spider is a giant of the spider world. Here it makes light work of a tree frog.

Killing Machine

A tree frog's mating call means one thing to a wandering spider. The spider feels the sound vibrations and knows that dinner is on the way!

A BUG WITH BITE

Strange but True

Imagine finding this huge South American wandering spider in your soup bowl! It measures nearly half a foot (15 cm) across.

Night and Day

A wandering spider has a busy nightlife. It hunts for frogs, lizards, and insects. But during the day, it takes it easy, spreads itself on a leaf, and dozes. Predators don't see the spider because it is so well camouflaged.

Eyes Front

Different types of wandering spiders have different arrangements of eyes, but they all have eight. In some kinds, the rows of eyes curve forward on the head, but in others they curve backward. Either way makes for perfect vision!

Spiders are experts in the art of poisoning. A spider releases venom through fangs that look like curved claws at the end of its jaws.

Works every time!

Portia Spider

The Portia spider is a real cannibal. It creeps into another spider's web and tugs on the silk. The web spider crawls toward the intruder, thinking it has trapped an insect. Then the Portia spider attacks, kills, and eats the surprised web spider.

DINNERTIME!

A spider stuns or kills an insect with venom from its needle-sharp fangs.

fangs

Then, it spits a cocktail of juices over the insect to turn it to pulp.

Finally, the spider sucks the insides out of the insect, leaving just its hard, crunchy casing.

The venom that shoots through a spider's fangs is far more poisonous than snake venom.

Tell Me Why

SPIDERS ARE FUSSY ABOUT THEIR FOOD

A banana spider's favorite food isn't bananas, it's the cockroaches that live on bananas. The banana spider eats little else, so people use it to help keep down the cockroach population.

A nighttime hunter like this spider just loves wood lice. The spider pierces the wood louse's tough exoskeleton with its enormously long fangs, so that it can get at the juicy body inside.

Danger! Deadly Spiders

Most spiders are poisonous. But don't worry, most spider bites won't harm you. There are, however, a few nasty biters that are dangerous.

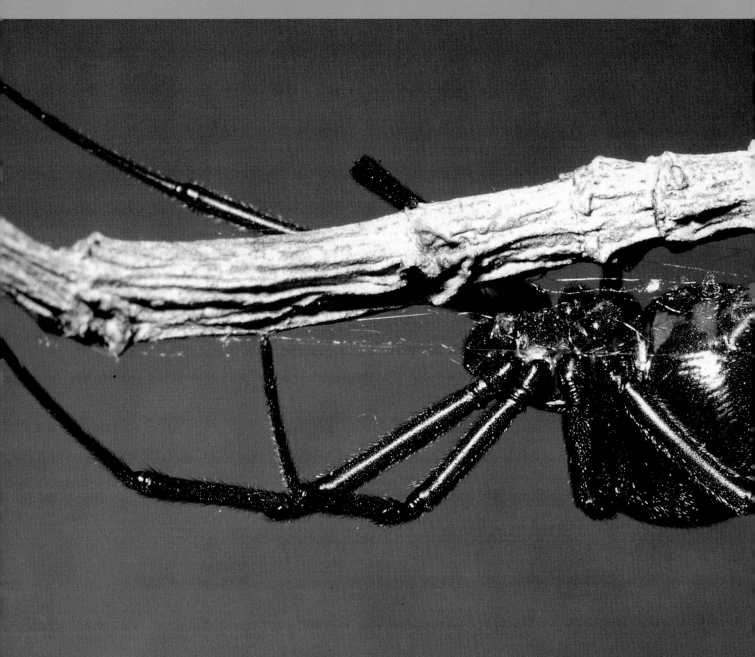

▲ The female black widow spider is about the size of an adult's thumbnail and highly poisonous.

Strange but True

Around the world, black widow spiders have different names, including hourglass spiders, and shoe-button spiders!

Black Widows

The black widow spider is a shy and retiring creature. It will bite only when it feels its life is threatened and would rather run away. But accidents happen because it finds shelter in shoes and clothes. One small bite is enough to kill.

Danger Down Under

The Australian funnel web spider wanders around back gardens in search of dinner. If it is disturbed, it will attack and deliver a harmful bite that's strong enough to pierce your fingernail. Victims may even die!

That's Weird

The deadly violin spider has a mark on its body that looks like a violin. Usually, its bite isn't fatal, but the wound can take a long time to heal and leave a large scar.

Hairy Knees

Imagine finding a big, hairy spider like this in your bath! But don't be scared, it wouldn't harm you.

△ This bird-eating spider from Mexico has poor eyesight, but uses its legs to find and capture prey.

Terrifying Tarantula

Do you think big spiders are scary? In the past, people believed that the bites of large European tarantulas were responsible for many deaths. In fact, the wrong spider was blamed. The real culprit turned out to be a smaller spider—the black widow. It just goes to show, size isn't everything!

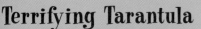

That's Weird

When people in Italy thought they had been bitten by a tarantula, they performed a lively dance called the tarantella. They believed that jumping around would make them better.

On the Defensive

SECRET WEAPONS

Spiders are always on the lookout for prey, but predators are also on the lookout for spiders. Clever disguises and quick getaways keep spiders out of trouble.

Good Disguise

Many spiders keep safe by looking exactly like leaves. The spiders are mottled to match bark or moldy leaves, green to match living leaves, or even have brown, crinkled outlines to look like dead leaves!

Spider Spears

Many big, hairy spiders shoot clouds of hairs into the faces of predators. The tiny hairs are sharp with hooked ends. They cause so much irritation that the spider has plenty of time to run away.

Rotten Disguise

Some spiders avoid dangerous predators by disguising themselves as bird droppings. One kind of bird-dropping spider even spins specks of white silk around itself on a leaf. This makes it look like a fresh dropping.

HA HA! What does a spider eat for breakfast? Flied eggs. HEE HEE!

Alien Bug

If you were a hungry predator, would you eat something that looked like a spaceship? The buffalo spider has a flat body, spiky spines, and bright colors. Would-be predators can't figure out what they've come across.

Strange but True

A spider from Madagascar disguises itself by hiding on a twig. It looks just like a dried-up bud.

That's Weird

A South American tree-dwelling spider leaves its enemies all wet. It simply raises its rear end toward its attacker and squirts liquid in its face.

23

A Date with Danger

When courting, the first thing a male spider does is to persuade the female spider not to eat him!

Strange but True

To escape the grip of a fierce female, a male spider may even leave behind some of his legs.

HA HA! HEE HEE!

What do you call recently married spiders? Newly webs.

⚠ This rather anxious male spider is more than three times smaller than the female!

That's Weird

A few male and female spiders are friendly to one another. One will tug on the web to let the other one know it wants to meet, then they play "pat-a-cake" with each other's legs.

Perfect Present

One type of wolf spider knows that the way to reach a female spider's heart is through her stomach! He presents his mate with a gift of a wrapped fly. While the female munches her meal, the male mates with her. He knows that as long as she is busy eating her present, she won't eat him!

I think she likes me.

One kind of water spider announces he's on his way to a female by sending drum beats across the water. Then he pulls on her dragline, rowing himself across the water to meet her. They strike up a romantic conversation by tapping each other's legs.

Message of Love

Many kinds of male spiders wave their long, hairy legs at female spiders to show they want to get to know them, not to be eaten for dinner! Some of these dance sequences can be complicated and involve all kinds of tricky steps—especially when you've got eight legs!

A kind of fishing spider finds an area of pond where a female spider has set up house. The male finds the female by following the fragrant scent she has left on the water.

Growing Up...

Some female spiders take great care of their eggs, wrapping them in a bubble of silk called an egg sac.

...Leaving Home

▲ A female wandering spider takes care of her egg sac. Many other spiders abandon their eggs.

A Good Start

Eggs hatch into spiderlings. Burrowing spiderlings are doted on by their mother, who takes care of their every need. But lots of other spiderlings have to fend for themselves. When food is short and they are hungry, they even eat each other!

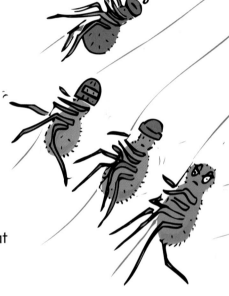

High Flyers

Some spiders take to the skies, especially young spiderlings that travel long distances to find a home of their own. They rise up to heights of 5,000 feet (1,525 m), flying on silken threads that catch the breeze! This is called "ballooning."

A SPLITTING TIME

Every time a spider gets too big for its skin, it just grows a brand-new one.

Ooops—I'm splitting up!

First, a split appears across the spider's back. The split grows and grows.

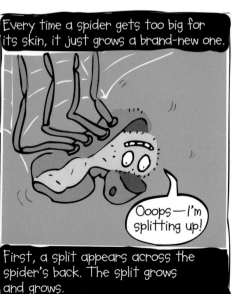

Phew!

Soon, the spider wriggles free of its old skin. This is called molting.

The spider hangs around a bit for the new skin to dry, then flexes its legs in anticipation of its new look!

I just love my new skin!

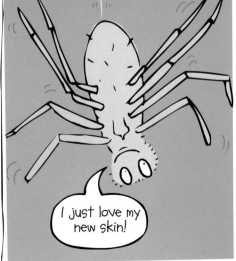

Spider Stories

Around the world, there are hundreds of stories about spiders, from hairy, scary monster spiders to spiders as the origins of life on Earth.

MONSTER SPIDER...CRAWLING TERROR 100 FEET

TARANTU

△ Imagine being attacked by towering tarantulas! Killer spiders were the gruesome inspiration behind this Hollywood film of the 1950s.

Spider-Man

A spider has special grip pads on its feet which give it the ability to walk up walls and across ceilings. This amazing feat was the inspiration behind the cartoon character Spider-Man. He can "weave a web as strong as steel" to catch his enemies, too.

Ceiling Thomas

In West Africa, the rascally hero of many stories is half-man, half-spider. He's called Anansi. When things are going his way, Anansi is a man, but when he's in trouble, he turns into a spider and hides on the ceiling—a habit which earned him the nickname of Ceiling Thomas.

He'll never find me here.

That's Weird

"Little Miss Muffet who sat on a tuffet," was a real person. Her father was a spider expert who insisted she ate mashed spiders. Until 200 years ago, this was thought to be a cure for the common cold.

29

Bad Guys
and Good Guys

There are over 30,000 kinds of spiders crawling about. Some people hate them, others keep them as pets. So, are spiders good guys or bad guys? Here are more amazing facts to help you decide...

It's a Set Up!

Most spiders, like this wolf spider, are harmless, but they're often blamed for other bugs' bites. The real culprits are usually blood-thirsty ticks or fleas, too small to see. The bugs quickly depart, leaving a nearby spider to be blamed for a crime it didn't commit.

Wonder Webs

Spider webs could help to save people's lives. The US Defense Department is attempting to use stretchy spider silk to make bullet-proof vests. The steel-like threads are strong enough to absorb the power of a flying bullet. Wow!

In New Guinea, there are giant wood spiders that spin webs 6 feet (2 m) wide. The huge, sticky traps are so tough, the people who live there use them as fishing nets!

Mean Machine

A Brazilian wandering spider must be the meanest spider on Earth. It hides away in people's homes and it won't think twice about giving a fatal bite. You can't even scare it away. If you hit the fearless fiend, it will try even harder to bite!

Holy Spiders

Some people believe spiders have special powers. In Polynesia, it's said that you reach heaven by climbing a giant ladder of spider silk that stretches up into the sky.

Spiders Save the World

Would you like to share your home with this leggy visitor? A house spider, like most spiders, is harmless and does a great job of killing flies and other insects that spread disease. Each year, spiders eat thousands of tons of dangerous bugs. Yeuch!

Index and Glossary

arachnid, 2

banana spider, 17
bird-dropping spider, 22
bird-eating spider, 20
black widow spider, 18, 19, 21
buffalo spider, 23
burglar spider, 13
burrow, 4, 6, 7
A hole or tunnel under the ground where some spiders live.

camouflage, 15
The patterns or colors that help an animal to look like its surroundings and hide from its enemies.
cave spider, 5
crab spider, 3

dragline, 8, 25
A strand of silk that a spider trails behind its body.

egg sac, 26
A furry pouch in which a female spider lays her eggs.
exoskeleton, 17
A bony covering on the outside of a spider's body.

fang, 2, 16, 17
A sharp, hollow claw that a spider uses to inject venom into its prey.
fishing spider, 13, 25
funnel web spider, 19

giant wood spider, 30

hammock weaver spider, 11
house spider, 31

jumping spider, 12

net-throwing spider, 10

orb spider, 11

Portia spider, 16
predator, 15, 22, 23
An animal that hunts and kills other animals for food.
prey, 2, 4, 5, 7, 8, 9, 12, 13, 20, 22
An animal that is hunted and eaten by other animals.

silk, 2, 5, 6, 8, 9, 10, 11, 16, 22, 26
spiderling, 27
A baby spider.

spinneret, 2
The part of a spider that produces silk.
spitting spider, 13

tarantula, 4, 21, 28
trapdoor spider, 6, 7, 27
tree-dwelling spider, 23
tropical spined spider, 23

venom, 16, 17
The poisonous liquid that a spider injects into prey with its fangs.
violin spider, 19

wandering spider, 14, 15, 26, 31
water spider, 5, 25
web, 2, 5, 10, 11, 13, 16, 25, 30
wolf spider, 13, 25, 30

Illustrations: Phillip Morrison
Consultant: Jonathan Elphick
Author: Christine Morley
Photographs: Front Cover: Natural History Photographic Agency; p1: Oxford Scientific Films; p3: Bruce Coleman Ltd; p4/5: Science Photo Library; p6/7: BBC Natural History Unit Picture Library; p8: Science Photo Library; p9: Planet Earth Pictures; p10: Planet Earth Pictures; p12/13: Oxford Scientific Films; p14/15: Premaphotos Wildlife; p16/17: Planet Earth Pictures; p18/19: Planet Earth Pictures; p20/21: Science Photo Library; p22: Science Photo Library; p23: Bruce Coleman Ltd; p24: BBC Natural History Unit Picture Library/Premaphotos Wildlife; p26: Premaphotos Wildlife; p27: Planet Earth Pictures; p28: The Kobal Collection/Universal; p29: Spider-Man: TM & © 1998 Marvel Characters, Inc. All Rights Reserved; p30: Natural History Photographic Agency; p31: Planet Earth Pictures.

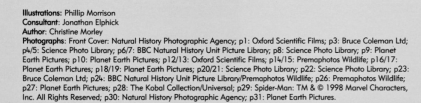